THE POLITICAL GAME

ENGAGE AND TRANSFORM YOUR LIFE FROM APATHY
TO EMPOWERMENT

JOHN THIBAULT

OFFICIAL BOOK TRAILER

The Political Game - Official Book Trailer

The Political Game

There is no excuse for whining about legal situations now that you have a guide to put your desired changes into motion.

— REVIEWED BY DANIEL D STAATS FOR READERS'
FAVORITE

To the point. Excellent information.

— KINDLE CUSTOMER

Don't just read the book but study and follow its instructions.

— MBAEBIE BUCHI

For permission requests, write to
"Permissions Coordinator"
iLobby LLC
325 Sharon Park Drive, #210
Menlo Park, CA 94025
http://www.ilobbyco.com

First edition, June 2018
The iLobby logo is a registered trademark of iLobby LLC.
The 5-3-5 Framework and the V3SM V3 Story Model are Trademarks of iLobby LLC.

❋ Created with Vellum

DISCLAIMER

This book is for educational purposes only and does not constitute an alternative to legal or other professional services advice. The publisher and author make no representations or warranties with respect to the accuracy or completeness of the contents of this book and disclaim any liability to any party with respect to any loss, damage, or disruption caused, or alleged to have been caused, by errors, omissions, information or programs contained herein. Any resemblance to actual persons, either living or dead, businesses, companies, events, or locales is coincidental. References are provided for informational purposes only and do not constitute an endorsement of any websites or other sources.

Please watch this YouTube video.
Change a Law
Visit Facebook Fan Page

PREFACE

Politics is a game, and policy is the highest level of play.

Most people don't engage in it because they think it is complicated, expensive, and outside of their comfort zone. Of course, there are lots of other reasons as well.

But I think it is an exciting arena. If more players were involved from more teams, we would increase competition, level the playing field, see new candidate discovery and emergence, and find solutions to some of the most pressing wicked problems in the world.

It doesn't have to be done just by the experts. Experts don't have all the answers. But politicians need input from regular people who have boots on the ground and a closer understanding of the problems we face, creative folks who can come up with unique new solutions.

That is the purpose of this book, to help get you into the game. To show you that it does not have to be as difficult as it seems and to help you avoid the pitfalls that most people run into whenever they think of politics and centers of power.

So join me on this journey, Jump in, read, learn, try the exercises, and see if this is right for you.

The world needs your input, now more than ever.

John Thibault
 Founder, CEO iLobby
 Menlo Park, CA May 2018

DISCLAIMER

This book is for educational purposes only and does not constitute an alternative to legal or other professional services advice. The publisher and author make no representations or warranties with respect to the accuracy or completeness of the contents of this book and disclaim any liability to any party with respect to any loss, damage, or disruption caused, or alleged to have been caused, by errors, omissions, information or programs contained herein. Any resemblance to actual persons, either living or dead, businesses, companies, events, or locales is coincidental. References are provided for informational purposes only and do not constitute an endorsement of any websites or other sources.

Please watch this YouTube video.
   Change a Law
   Visit Facebook Fan Page

CONTENTS

Chapter 1   1
Chapter 2   5
Chapter 3   12
Chapter 4   16
Chapter 5   21
Chapter 6   26
Chapter 7   32

Review   37
Also by John Thibault   39
About the Author   41
About iLobby   43
Awards   45
Bonus Links   47
Free Stuff   49
Share Your Story   51

1

What if there was something that you really wanted to do that was meaningful, and you had a 30 percent chance of being able to complete it, but the upside was 200, 300, maybe 400 percent or more?

Yet what if this thing that you wanted to get done was really pretty hard or complicated, and you needed to have other people help you? Would you be willing to undertake it?

What if this project required vast resources, and you knew you would need the help of other people to be able to pay for it? Could you do it?

What if you knew some people were succeeding at this, but you just didn't understand how they could do it and maybe you even, sometimes, resented the fact that they were getting it done and you weren't.

You were being left out and what if when they got it done, the thing that they wanted, they then told you what to do and you had to obey them.

How would you feel about that?

Frustrated, disempowered, disengaged?

Well, that's what a lot of American voters feel.

They're interested in politics and how it shapes their life, but they're not really sure what policy is all about, and they think that's better left to someone else.

Maybe you think that you don't have the answers. Perhaps you think you don't have enough education or enough understanding, or you don't understand all the insider moves that need to happen? But what if you were wrong?

What am I talking about? I'm talking about political engagement.

I know it sounds boring for most of you.

You start thinking of things like the President, the Congress, the Constitution and the Democrat party versus the Republican Party, how difficult it is, dealing with bureaucracies, and all of that.

You're right. There is incredible complexity to all of it, but think about this. There are a lot of complicated things in our lives, and when we need to deal with them, we bring in experts.

We can't know everything. We can't do everything, and in the arena of politics, it's one area where we have neglected to understand that there are people who can help us out.

Now, this doesn't apply to all of us. You may be reading this and say, well, that doesn't apply to me because, at my company, we have people who handle that for us. In all likelihood, you work for a large company, and the company has a government relations department, sometimes called government affairs. They work with the executives, the CEO of the company, policymakers, lawmakers, lobbyists, attorneys, local civic leaders, state senators, well, in fact, the entire political spectrum.

They know the rules. They understand the legislative calendar. They know who is sitting on what committees. They know the difference between campaign finance and grassroots campaigning.

And for the most part, none of us are taught these things in school. So no wonder we feel left out.

We don't understand the language. The complexity baffles us. There are so many issues, many opinions, and so many arguments on both sides. It's hard to discern what the right answer is, and we don't know what the implications are for something as significant as policy, particularly at the federal level. But even when you bring it down to the state or the local level or your local school board, you find that you need to get versed on the issues and dive in deeply to really have a sense of what it means.

THAT'S where most of us fall off, and when I say most of us, I'm talking about 95 percent of the population.

There's probably another three or four percent who are somewhat engaged and understand a fair amount of this. I would say there is less than one percent of the population who is actively politically involved and very clear about what their agenda is, what they want to get done, how to do it, who to engage, when to join, what the risks are, what the timeline is, and why they should even bother.

THE PURPOSE of this book is to show you why it matters.

If you never get involved, if you don't have a seat at the table, it's unlikely that your voice will be heard. It's doubtful that your opinions will count or that your ideas even matter. This isn't just about the simple act of voting. This is about taking an active interest in your political life, in the political life of your family, your community, your business, your town, maybe even your state and the country.

What I want to show you is that there is a way to engage. There is a way to become informed. It doesn't have to take up all of your time.

WHEN YOU SUCCEED, the benefits can be tremendous. Are you game?

If so, let's go on this journey together, and I guarantee you that if you read the material and do the exercises, at the end of seven days, your mindset will be transformed.

You will move from apathy to engagement, from ignorance and frustration to inside knowledge and empowerment.

If you want more control of your political life, this is your opportunity to jump on board and make a difference. Make a difference that really counts and makes a difference in the world.

I n the late seventies, I graduated from one of the top film schools in the country with a dream of becoming a successful screen-writer and director. In fact, it was everybody's dream.

We all thought we had a message of inspiration, but in reality, we were young, and we did not know what the message was. We just knew we wanted to make a difference. Like everybody else, I believed the way to do that was to influence people emotionally and through film.

The years went by, Jimmy Carter left office, President Reagan came into power, and I kept writing one screenplay after another and looking to raise money with a business partner. It dragged on like this year after year, and every year, we got a little bit closer. Every year, we thought this would be the one, and we came close several times to what I thought would become a million-dollar deal.

The big break!

To support this habit, I worked as a story analyst. I then did some temporary and other consulting work for the studios in different departments, Development, P.R., Production. It gave me exposure to being on the lot at the major studios, and my agent felt that this would be beneficial because I was mingling. I had screenplays optioned, and I was out there. Any day the big break would come.

Other friends and a roommate quickly ended up becoming creators of well-known television shows and writing novels. They went on to moderate and, in some cases, reasonably big successes. I kept thinking my day would come, but I became frustrated and eventually exasperated by the whole process.

Then one day, one short-term consulting gig turned into a longer-term official offer. It sounded appealing at the time, but I realized I knew nothing about the area. It was in government affairs at a major studio. Government affairs? What's that?

I was told it was fairly high level, that we would be dealing with senators, congressmen, heads of state, the executives at the studio. We had an internal PAC (a political action committee), and aside from the long hours, we would have broad policy exposure to Washington and Sacramento.

So I accepted the position and realized I could still write in the evenings and on weekends. Most of the political activity was during the day except for fundraisers and special events.

It must have been through osmosis, but I found the experience pretty enriching, intellectually stimulating. Although I was not getting my scripts sold, I was getting great exposure to some of the biggest power centers in the country: the entertainment industry and Washington.

The issues in the air at the time were everything from trade policy to intellectual property theft to union negotiation permits for filming. We lived through the Rodney King riots, the Northridge Earthquake, the increasing violence in the early nineties in L.A., and other challenges.

But a startling thing happened a month after my father passed away, a sniper shooting on the black tower where I worked in North Hollywood in April of 1993. Bullets flew through the large pane glass windows of the fifth floor and pierced the walls behind me. I crawled out of there and made my way to the center of the building near the elevator shafts, yet the sound of gunshots seemed like it was coming from every direction. I remember thinking I work in a gated studio and live in a safe neighborhood, yet no matter what, my life could have ended there.

My wife and I decided we needed a safer place. We needed to move away. And so we did. We spent the next three years in Boulder, Colorado, where I started a children's software company focused ironically on violence-free software. But somehow moving into multimedia then proved to be the wrong timing. There was a greater force coming on the scene. Technology and media were transforming, and we sensed the change. It was this disruptive thing called the Internet.

After a few safe years of living in Boulder, I realized we had to get back into the action.

I interviewed with dozens of companies in L.A., San Francisco, and New York, and eventually, found this unique little opportunity with a seven-person San Jose startup that was doing online auctions.

My wife said to me at the time, "Auctions? You know nothing about auctions." And I said, "That's right. It's perfect." Because I had known nothing about government affairs either and I did very well. But that little company took off, dominated the market, and became a global enterprise, eBay.

A few more years passed, and I joined another little startup in the financial space. This company was providing financial advice to companies and individuals in the defined benefit and defined contribution arena. Most of the senior guys were PhDs in finance. I was a consumer marketing guy at this time with a background and a masters in film.

Once again, my wife said to me, "You know nothing about finance." And I once again said, "That's right. It's perfect. I knew nothing about auctions. I knew nothing about policy and politics and I knew nothing about finance. That's why it's perfect."

They seemed to agree. Even the Nobel laureate, Bill Sharpe, who had founded the company, Financial Engines, was glad to have me on board.

So I made the transition from the entertainment industry to the tech world with a smattering of politics along the way. It was this triangulated Venn diagram of the companies I worked for that brought me to the point where I realized one of the next major challenges we were all facing had to do with policy and politics.

By now, I personally knew several people who ran for office and assisted some of them with their campaigns, which they won.

I knew others who launched much bigger campaigns. Some won, some did not, but in the end, what I found was as they transitioned from corporate America into the world of politics, they often ran across the same problems that we all do, focusing on campaign finance, focusing on candidates, not being clear on the issues, not being able to clearly enunciate what their message was, and then not being able to connect with the voter.

No different from what we experience when someone writes a screenplay for a movie, and they cannot connect with their audience.

But this hadn't been my experience when I worked in L.A. I found that we were successful in dealing with the politicians.

In fact, the chairman of MCA/Universal at the time, Lew Wasserman, had maintained significant relationships with every U.S. Administration going back to the Kennedy administration, and one of the lessons he learned was the following. You can't control the government, so you have to make friends with it.

You don't want to work against the government. You want to work with it, and one of the underlying lessons that people often miss is that, and I used to ask this question, what causes people to engage?

Is it when they have nothing to lose or something to gain? Or is it when the risk of loss can occur? I think that's closest to the mark.

When you have a family, a wife, and children, you become

concerned with issues around your community, homeownership, education.

When you own a business, you are concerned about regulations, city ordinances, taxes, transportation for employees, affordable housing, infrastructure. As your interests grow outside of your own immediate needs, and you realize you have a payroll to meet, you have employees, and you have a board of directors and investors. Then your concerns become national and often global in nature. That's why companies at the highest level of performance are engaged in public policy.

But does that mean it has to stay that way?

Only top CEOs of fortune 500 companies can talk or think about political change, policy issues, and matters that affect the country? No.

I think one of the fundamental problems is, we know that information doubles every year to year and a half. We know that we're living in an accelerating economy, and we know that the politicians do not have all the answers nor do the think tanks, the universities, the special interests, and so-called experts.

So who has answers to some of the biggest problems we are facing?

Often it is the people on the ground, but their voices are not being heard, and when they're not heard, eventually they just give up. They don't even try anymore, and that's what I saw happening.

I did not see it when I worked in government affairs. They cared. They were effective, they persisted, and they maintained relationships with lawmakers.

So, in fact, as promised, when I first joined, yes, we would meet with senators and congressmen. We would have heads of state come in for private dinners.

I attended the homes of studio heads and studio executives who courted the politicians like royalty and vice versa, but there was open dialogue. There were collaborative communications, and the entertainment industry had been at this a long time. What I noticed was it wasn't until the mid-to-late nineties that the booming tech industry became more dominant, they could not stay isolated in Silicon Valley. Tech companies needed to deal with Washington, and that became more and more apparent as time went on.

So what did they do? Did they protest in the streets? No. Did they march on the Washington Mall? No. Did they burn police cars to get their point across? No. Did they blow up buildings? No. Did they call talk radio? Maybe. Did they write up ads in the Wall Street Journal? The New York Times? Sometimes. Did they take out ads in the major press? Occasionally. Did they contribute to various campaigns for members of Congress? Yes, often, they did.

And we were asked to as well. But did they really understand the power of committees? Did they really understand the power of the committee structure and constituent alignment? Did they really follow the rules of the Senate or the House of Representatives? Did they really appreciate the tenure, the pace, the calendar of Washington and the state capitols? Probably not.

WHAT I WANT to share with you is the journey I went on as I was exposed to all these changes and realized that there is a way to solve individual problems. There is a way to engage average citizens and small businesses to begin to accept the challenge of becoming involved in policymaking at the local, state, or federal levels.

With the increasing speed, complexity, and change we're facing, we need new voices. We need to hear from more people. We need to solve problems more quickly. We need to take old laws off the books.

We need to institute new laws that are keeping pace with technological changes around drones, space law, genetics, nanotechnology, and more.

Washington and the state capitals use technology and methods that have been around for hundreds of years. Some companies have made small inroads and offered a baseline of technology to improve certain things. Still, many government departments have not yet caught up. The question I wanted to answer was, "Why does it take so long to get a law changed?" I think you can guess.

Why do politicians run for office, campaign on one platform, make promises, and then once they're in office, they reverse themselves? The voters and the donors who helped them get in are often frustrated and disappointed because what they thought they would do just never happens.

So how can we have our kids believe in the country and our leaders, and become more involved in politics without canvassing door-to-door, licking stamps or stuffing envelopes?

I think they want more than that. I think they want to make a meaningful contribution.

I think they want to say, and I think you do too, "I need to do more."

That's the point of this book, to take you through step-by-step in seven days, the challenges you face about getting clear on setting policy in a minimal way, but in a way that you might think of like a fractal.

What you do at the local level can expand to the county, state, national, or even global level.

So sit tight. Let's jump in together, and I will walk you through what it takes to become a citizen legislator.

3

I n Washington, as in Hollywood, everything starts with an idea.

IN HOLLYWOOD, it's referred to as a concept, or preferably a "high concept" that you can write on the back of a napkin. That's what they say anyway.

In Silicon Valley, it's an elevator pitch. If you want to raise money for your company, you should be able to describe it in one sentence, seven words, and it should be incredibly engaging.

In the world of politics, it starts with an idea, and that idea is called an issue.

The question you get asked is, what's your issue? And the problem could be anything. It could be national defense, immigration, health care, women's rights, gun control, education, infrastructure, space law, taxes, corporate regulation.

In fact, the US Senate uses 76 issue codes to classify these activities, and it is these codes that lobbyists use when they describe the area of activity they're working on.

I should just say that when I describe Washington, I'm also refer-ring to the state capitals and the local level. However, at the state and local level, much of this is simplified. The issues aren't precisely the same. Some of them overlap, some don't, but the idea is pretty much the same. If you want to get something done in DC, you have to know what your issue is.

Once you describe it, the next thing you need to do is you need to know your position.

Think about the words that go with this. What's your position? Where do you stand on this issue? Are you on the left, the right, or the center?

Together, the issue and your position really tell you what you are for and what you are against. So if you are for something, you want to get something done. If you are against something, you want to stop something from happening. Simple!

If you think about it, for most of us, there are probably two or three issues we care about, and they are usually related to things in our life. But just like you have technology companies solving prob-lems in areas where they see something that needs to be improved or in the case of entertainment, they create a hero with a problem who wants to overcome an opponent, the same things and often the same rules apply.

In the case of policy, you have an issue. Still, the question really is a broad description of an area you're interested in that has a particular problem. Some of these issues are economic, some are social, some are simple, and some are complex. Usually, when you have special interest groups, they are battling on both sides or one side against the other. Just like in a football game. It's a competition of ideas. The question becomes, who has the right answer to a wicked problem?

The tricky part is that nobody knows for sure.

.   .   .

THERE ARE ALWAYS UNINTENDED CONSEQUENCES. So if you follow this analogy for a moment, you can see how laws, like software code, end up with bugs and need to have user testing done and often need to be modified and updated, but often are not.

So we live with lousy code, outdated laws, harmful regulations, and frustration where an Act that got passed 20 or 30 or 40 years ago no longer applies to our current situation. But nobody's going back in there to fix it because it hasn't come up and the only time it does come up is if there's a court case.

So these problems move from the legislative branch where they're initially decided to the executive branch where they're implemented and enforced, and then to the judicial arena where they are adjudicated and looked at in terms of what the law says, what the precedents are.

So HERE'S a 15-second version of the government structure. We have three bodies of government, three co-equal branches: the legislative, the executive, and the judicial. What I'm focusing on here is the legislative branch because, for the average person, that is your point of entry. That is your point of access. You have a representative in Congress, and that's whom you can go to with your issue.

IF YOU'RE in Hollywood and you want to sell a screenplay, you need an agent. If you're in Silicon Valley, and you want to fund your company, you need an introduction to an angel or a venture capitalist. If you're in Washington and you want to get a law passed, you need a bill sponsor.

The sponsor is the lawmaker who is going to take your idea, turn it into legislative bureau language, write it up for you and introduce it on the floor.

At the end of this chapter, and throughout this book, we have a series of exercises for you to get clear on your issue.

What I want you to do is look at the issues that are available, or an issue that you have; categorize it and name it at the end of this chapter.

Go ahead and do the exercise.

List your issue; write up one short sentence about what it is, and then list your position.

We'll have a link to an exercise workbook and some videos that should help you out.

LINKS

6 Things Politicians Want to Know - Video
   6 Reasons Why Congress Won't Listen To You - PDF

4

Okay, great.

Now, you have an issue, and you know your position.

The next thing I want you to do is to write it on a piece of paper and format it. I'll explain.

At the very top is your issue. Right below is the sentence on the top of the horizontal line forming a "T."

Then in the center, draw a vertical line that comes down. You're dividing your paper in half, to the left and the right. Now you know your position. Your dominant position is going to be on one side or the other. Let's say it's on the left side, and let's say that it is the pro or positive side.

I want you to make five short bullet points about why this is important. Just brainstorm it quickly and pick your issue and say, what are the top five things that will convince someone that you are right? Take your time. If you get more than five, that's fine, but five is enough just to get going.

So go ahead, take a moment and write down five points on the left side of the paper in bullet point form why this issue matters, and you have the right point of view.

· · ·

OKAY, after you've done that, I want you to take your pro hat off and go to your con hat. Put that on, go to the right-hand side of the paper, which is the negative side, and I want you to argue against yourself. List several points as well.

But I'm not going to ask you to do five. I'm only going to ask you to do three. So I want you to come up with three points of view or three ideas or three arguments that would go against what you're trying to get done that would be logical, and sound. Really undermine what you're trying to do so it wouldn't pass.

Go ahead, take a few minutes and do that, and I'll include a sample below with a link for you to see how we do it here.

GOOD. Now, continue on. At the very bottom, what I want you to do is pick five people or groups or politicians who might support the idea that you're proposing.

Okay?

If you don't know anyone specifically, you can just list a general description.

So, for instance, if your issue has to do with immigration and you have five points on why your position is the right one and three on why the opposition is wrong, then list below five groups who would support you.

Let's say your dominant position is pro-immigration in a certain kind of way, and I'm not specifying what those arguments would be for you. I want you to come up with them, but basically, you're creating a framework here. So below that, you're going to list five supportive groups.

"5-3-5 Framework"™

Issue	
(+) PRO	(-) CON
1. Argument	1. Argument
a) Fact 1	a) Fact 1
b) Fact 2	b) Fact 2
2. Argument	2. Argument
a) Fact 3	a) Fact 3
b) Fact 4	b) Fact 4
3. Argument	3. Argument
4. Argument	
5. Argument	

1. Supporters	4. Supporters
2. Supporters	5. Supporters
3. Supporters	

ONE GROUP COULD BE a pro-immigration law group, or religious group, even if you don't know precisely who they are. And then other groups who you know support the position that you are putting up.

Go ahead, take a few minutes, and do that.

OKAY? Let's look at what you have. What you have mostly is a framework.

You have what I call a "5-3-5 Framework." You have an issue, you have a clear position, and you have five arguments on the left side in favor of your position. You have three arguments on the right side going against it and undermining your position. Then you have five groups of supporters who would support you and agree with you in terms of what you're trying to get done. Great! Good job.

NOW, these five points are actually arguments.

I want you to think about it in those terms because if you ever hear politicians talk, that's how they speak. A reporter might ask, "What is your position on immigration?" And they will say, "Well, I approve of X, or I voted for a particular bill H.R. 1234 that supported this, or I believe that a certain group has the right point of view and they have these arguments and I believe those arguments are worthy and that we should vote on them."

So they're basically using the statement of... here's my issue, here's my position, and here are the arguments in support.

The good part is if you include the opposite as well, what you're doing is you're allowing an individual to know that you have spent some time thinking about this. You know what the opposition might say. So it puts you in a better light because you could easily say, "Listen, here's what I'd like to get done. Here's the reason why, but some people on the other side would say A, B, and C, the negative arguments, and they could be right. Still, I have a counter-argument or a rebuttal to what they're saying because they don't have all the facts or they don't understand the issue well enough. Or their arguments are off-topic and unrelated to what my specific issue is because they're not addressing what it is."

And what that shows is that you have done your homework. You have a balanced approach.

What you've accomplished by using this framework, the "5-3-5 Framework," is you've gotten well past a slogan. You are not standing up, holding up a sign saying IMMIGRATION FOR ALL or JUSTICE FOR ALL or BUILD THE WALL or down with integration or up with whatever it might be.

I'm trying to be very general here without planting ideas in your head. Still, you're not coming away as a person who just has a sing-song slogan, a one-track mind, a stubborn single-issue focus, or someone bashing the president's behavior.

You're coming away as a thoughtful individual who has looked at a problem, and you're beginning to build an intellectual framework that politicians understand.

AND THAT's the whole point of what you want to get done.

So when you start dealing with policy, ideas, and changing laws, whether it's at the local, state, or federal level, you're going to go through the same exercise.

If you don't do it, the politician, the staff, the lobbyists, they're all doing this anyway. They may not be doing it explicitly, but they're definitely doing the kind of work that we're talking about here, and you see it on the back end.

When a politician is interviewed, they say, "What did you like about the bill?" The media may ask them that question, and they'll answer, "Well, I agree with this amendment on this particular area, and we like the bill that came out by senator so and so, and we think that this is a good bill that came out of the House and we voted for it, but there were portions of it that we just couldn't get behind."

All of a sudden, you might hear those conversations and begin to understand that they're talking about the specific arguments or the areas of support or rebuttal related to the issue and how it's going to be moved forward.

I'm not asking you to draft a bill. I'm not asking you to go into specific language. All I'm saying is think about the one word for your issue. Then add one little sentence about what it really means.

Then select an example of what your position is in terms of are you on the left or right? The positive or the negative?

Do you want something, or do you want to stop something from happening?

And then develop five key points to support that. These are your arguments. Add three more, to undermine what you're getting done, and then brainstorm five groups, people, or politicians who might support what you're trying to get done.

Congratulations!

You made significant headway if you got this far.

LINKS

6 Things Politicians Want to Know - Video

6 Reasons Why Congress Won't Listen To You - PDF

5

During the Second World War, it had become common knowledge that some Japanese Americans were interned in camps in California and elsewhere when we were at war with Japan, Germany, Italy, and the Axis powers. What a lot of people didn't know was, it wasn't just the Japanese who were put into camps. It also happened to Italian Americans and other groups.

But the story I want to share with you is a story of a young 12-year-old boy at the time whose father and uncles were Italian-American citizens. They lived in San Jose, and their rights and people they knew were suspended near the end of the war. They were subject to a curfew. Some lost their jobs and their homes, others had their boats confiscated, and still, others were put into camps.

For 50 years, this was kept hidden from the general public. It was considered to be classified information. But by 2010, these stories started to come out, and Chet Campanella, who is now 86 years old, asked the State of California for an apology for having committed the acts. Ultimately, the State agreed.

The way he got that to happen was, he entered a contest that had been set up and sponsored by then California State Senator Joe Simit-

ian, who held a contest open to constituents in his district called
There Oughta' Be a Law.

But Chet took it a step further.

Not only did he get an apology from the State of California, he
then decided he wanted to go to his local Congresswoman in San Jose,
representative Zoe Lofgren. He had received some local press, which
animated him. In paragraph form, he presented the simple facts
around what had happened to the Congresswoman. She was shocked.
Most politicians were.

They were embarrassed and unaware that this had happened. So
she and her staff drafted language for him and created two bills that
are currently in the 115th Congress. They are H.R. 1706 and H.R.
1707, the mistreatment of Italian-Americans during the Second
World War.

What he asked for is $3 million to educate Americans about the
incident from over 50 years ago and an apology from the federal
government.

The two bills have been referred to committee, which is where
they are now; the House Judiciary and House Education and the
Workforce committees.

One thing that most of us don't realize is that, on average, during a
two-year term in Congress, the House has about 10,000 bills. So we
have 435 members who are assigned to approximately 25 committees
to review the bills, decide if they move forward, vote on them, and
then bring them to the floor for a full House vote if warranted.

Then the same would have to happen in the Senate, and if passed,
they would have to be signed by the President to become law.

In this case, these two bills are languishing in committee, as are
many other measures. Because there are so many other pressing bills
that Congress is dealing with, these might get short shrift.

BUT THE POINT I want to make is that an individual citizen took it
upon himself to draft simple language to present it to a lawmaker,
deal with them appropriately and civilly, and then ultimately work

with the government to get the bills in a form where they could go through the legislative chamber.

He didn't sign a petition, protest, march, or undertake other, less effective actions.

It's an encouraging story because if he can do it, you can too.

All Chet did was he picked an issue, something that was meaningful and personal to him, write it up, put it into a simple form and pursue it as doggedly as he could. But he had one thing working in his favor. And this is the next thing I'd like you to do as an exercise.

Yes, he had his issue, his position, and the arguments to support it on either side.

But he also had the facts, the stubborn truthful facts.

So after you list your arguments in the "5-3-5 T Framework" what I want you to do is make a few subpoints of facts, sources. Something that will back you up.

This could be data, videos, media reports, analytical reports, government analysis, or just stories from people who have perhaps given you some information.

DROP those in underneath your arguments. If you have a case, let's say you have those five points on the left-hand side, you get down to point number one. You say, okay, look, I know what this is, and I need a couple of supporting data points. You can easily find those, drop them in, and then you put the sources in.

Think of it as adding footnotes on a college paper or outline to support your main points. What you're looking for are facts.

Why are you doing this? Because if a lawmaker looks at it, they're going to want to know what the underlying sources are. Who is being affected, how many people are affected, what is the impact, what is the economic cost? How much will it cost to put this bill into place?

And the more you do that homework, the more it will help them understand what you're trying to get done and put you and your issue in a better light.

. . .

So, now you've got your "5-3-5- Framework" really humming along. You've got your "T" written up, and you have your issue at the top. You have the one sentence of what you want to get done. You've listed your five main arguments for what you want to get done on the left-hand side of that T, your three opposing arguments or rebuttals on the right side, and now you're listing some sub-points beneath each. These are factually going to back up what you are saying, so there is a reliable data source that anybody can go to and independently check.

Finally, below that, you have five groups who would support the entire idea. In Chet's case, he had the National Italian American Foundation out of Washington DC support and, therefore, there's a larger group who came to his aid and has been a good ally for him.

WHAT HAVE you accomplished so far? Think about it.

You have an understanding of how this works. You have a framework to go forward with. It didn't take that much time to get to this particular stage.

You have the issue, your position, the arguments, and the facts, and the next thing I'm going to touch on is one of the more compelling areas that people often neglect.

You might think if you just have all the arguments, all the facts, and it shows that someone is being harmed or you need to get this done, or there's a group who are going to benefit or why it's great, that's enough.

But sometimes, it isn't. It goes much farther.

Sometimes, you need to have a compelling emotional story that goes with it, and that's where we're going to go next.

What's your story?

LINKS

Chet Campanella Story - Blog and Video

6

There are a lot of political books on how to write a letter to your congressman, what the salutation should be, how you address them, how you send it. Do you send a fax? Do you send an email? Can you send a physical letter? Do you send it Federal Express? Should you approach your lawmaker at a town hall and pitch them on what you want to get done? Is it better to go to a city council meeting and just wait until 10:00 PM at night, get your two minutes to speak, and then be off?

All of these are things in terms of how you interact with government officials and lawmakers, but it really comes down to protocol.

Aside from what we've already talked about, one of the things is an element that people often overlook. But I don't want you to ignore this. And that is a compelling story.

So what is a story?

A story is an anecdote. A story is a personal recording of a series of events. Still, it's told in a certain kind of way, and what I want to do is layout three components that are in stories. I can say this from personal knowledge because these three components are in the best stories we see come out of Hollywood, movies, books, novels, and TV shows, but they can also apply here.

. . .

IN THE LAST CHAPTER, we summarized this, and I said, you have your issue, your position, and your arguments. But do you have a hero or what I will call a victor (on the assumption that you're going to win)?

If you're familiar with the writings of Joseph Campbell, he talks about the hero's journey. So I won't go into that here, but it's handy material for you to understand that you are doing the same thing.

You or someone you know will be the victor or the hero in this particular narrative. Imagine three circles. You have a victor in the upper left-hand ring. Then the person who is opposing you or the group who is opposed to you or the folks who don't want you to win, well, what do we call them? The villain. People think the villain is evil, but the best films are really strong, powerful, precise, and they represent the dark side of what it is that you're trying to get done.

I'll touch on immigration again because it's a great example.

Both sides, positive (+) and negative (-), think the other side is wrong, but the party in favor on the pro (+) team believes they have the right answer to a complex problem. Whereas the other side, the con (-) side which we'll call the villain, believe the pro side is entirely wrong, and the con side should be victorious.

I'm only using that so you can understand where the circles are. In either case, often what's happening is both the positive and the negative are trying to help somebody. Well, who are they trying to help?

They're trying to help the circle right below. And who is in that circle? It's the victim. Who are the victims? Well, historically, it's been someone weaker, defenseless, unable to take care of themselves. So often when we look at it, we see that it is sometimes young people, sometimes women, someone treated unfairly, exploited children, animals, the environment.

It can be human or animal or, in fact, nature.

And the way you present your case is by saying we're for the hero on the right side or we are the side representing a positive point of view and the villain is doing bad things, and we need to stop them. So we are proposing this law, bill, idea, issue to help them. We are supporting the victims because they can't do it for themselves.

When you don't have a victim, you just have the two sides battling it out. Then it looks like the victor or hero side appears self-serving. "We want to get this thing done," they say, "because it is good for us." And usually, what you'll hear is they will often say, "Well, it will create jobs in your district or in our community. We believe that by doing and building this plant in this area, we will create so many jobs. So if you, Mr. Politician, vote for this and give us a carve-out or amendment or promote this bill or sponsor this bill, then that will be good for the community."

It will obviously be suitable for the interests of the people pushing it or advocating for it. Still, they don't want to appear self-serving. So when you can come up with a powerful disinterested hero who is helping the underprivileged or the victim in this case against the evil villain, then you are creating an emotional context around your issue.

You are relaying a true story. Chet had these three elements going for him. He was an interested third party trying to right a wrong and help those who could not speak for themselves any longer. He had a villain, represented by the government during the Second World War.

A hero, a villain, and a victim. I sometimes refer to this as the "V3 Story Model;" victor, villain, and the victim.

V3 Story Model (V3SM)™

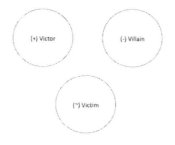

V3 Story Model - V3SM ™

IF YOU CAN BRING in real stories of harm to your narrative of how the negative side is actually hurting others, harming children, animals, the environment, the future, our economy, any of these things, you're going to have a more compelling and convincing case.

And this is where a lot of these bills fall apart. They don't have a human connection.

They don't have an emotional subtext. They don't have a story structure associated with them. So they seem entirely abstract. It just looks like here's a bond measure that we want to put through, it's going to cost this amount of money, nobody's going to be hurt, and it's going to do these good things. It's going to help us build roads, or it's going to create better infrastructure, those kinds of things, and it shouldn't have an impact on taxes or anything else.

When you look at those and read them, they just don't seem compelling, engaging, or believable.

Now, maybe there are underlying facts that support them. Perhaps there is an underlying story. Perhaps they have actual witnesses and people who would be harmed if certain legislation went forward or hurt if some bill did not go ahead. Maybe no one will uncover the unintended consequences for years to come.

But either way, if you can create a simple model with a positive hero (victor) or a Knight in shining armor or someone who is coming to the rescue of a victim (damsel in distress), whether it is the government or a particular group of people or a specific special interest group and they are saying that the other side (the evil monster) has it all wrong and this is why they are protecting it, you wind up with a better and more human story.

IT APPEALS to our sense of compassion, and we want to help move that forward.

Politicians are human, after all. They are no different from you and me, and they will respond to that as well. But it also gives them ammunition to talk about individual cases of how this legislation should be implemented, what it should do, and how it should move forward.

So to recap, you have the "5-3-5 Framework" as a structure to begin with. It shouldn't take you more than 15 or 20 minutes to come up with an issue that you really care about, figure out what side of the item you're on so that you know your position, plug in a few arguments to find some supporting data that will make it look like you've really done your homework, find a group that supports you and then drop it into the story structure (V3 Story Model) so that you can make a compelling case, bring in anecdotes, and real stories of why the thing that you're doing has to be done now.

It's essential to make it work. And when all this comes together, you are creating the basis for a really strong presentation. And that's what it's all about.

You want to be able to pull all this information together, and I'll talk about this next.

WHEN YOU PULL IT TOGETHER, you can actually deliver it in a 10 to 15-minute visit with your lawmaker. You can use it to persuade other people to join your cause or campaign. You can use it to get people to support your idea. You can use it to raise funds so that you will be able to continue to grow your base by getting your message out there and amplify your voice.

So go ahead, fill it in. Think about the story structure. Take a look at the samples that we have at the end of this chapter, and now that you have the structure, build something compelling and convincing.

You'll be far ahead of the rest of the crowd. And you've written it up with a simple framework that will not take more than one page and 15 minutes of your time. Finally, even if you don't do it for yourself, you might be helping someone else out for whom this really matters.

So give it a shot.

LINKS

6 Reasons Why Congress Won't Listen to You
    Free Online Tutorial

7

I f you've ever watched any commercials on television or listened to them on the radio, you will see a very similar structure that I'm going to point out right here.

Often they start with a problem, and they'll show you a few examples of the problem that we can all relate to. It's a statement of common belief.

For instance: *Most people don't like bugs. Bugs are biting us. They're terrible. We want to get rid of them. So here's the solution. We have a bug spray. The bug spray doesn't hurt anybody. It just kills the bugs. You have a problem. We have a solution.*

THEN THEY INTRODUCE the product and say, this is the product of choice because it provides these benefits. It does what we set out to do. It eliminates the problem. It kills the bugs, makes you happy, and everyone is feeling fine after this. And then they have the CTA or the call to action, and here it is.

So for $19.95, you can buy XYZ bug spray, and that will take care of everything. And if you act now in the next 15 minutes, you can get two *bottles plus a special container to put your bugs in, but you have to act now and call this number or go to this website or pull out your credit card.*

That's the call-to-action. In politics, it's not called a call-to-action. They refer to it as an "Ask."

LET'S say you've done the complete framework. You've rehearsed it, and you could pull it off in 10 to 15 minutes. At the end of it, the lawmaker is going to say, "Well, what can I do for you?" If you're a professional, you will say that this is what you would like them to do. This is the "ask." You are asking them to vote for your issue, sponsor a bill or to sponsor legislation that you're bringing to their attention or if they're not in a position or on the right committee to help out, you're asking them if they wouldn't mind writing a "Dear Colleague" letter to the member who is the chairman or chairwoman of the committee related to the issue that you want to get done.

The ask is straightforward. It is expected. This is not a quid pro quo.

You are not talking about money in exchange for anything. It's a request from a constituent. That's you.

You're describing a problem in your community, and you're presenting a solution. You're showing that other people support you. You are thoughtfully giving the lawmaker and their staff evidence of what your research has revealed to you. You're showing that you know how both sides work. You're showing that there are groups who support you, and perhaps there are groups who oppose you, and you know about them as well. And then you're giving a couple of anecdotes or a personal story about why this is the right thing to do.

That is the story that you put together.

And finally, you're saying to them, so what I would like you to do, Dear Congressman or Dear Senator is to support this legislation because that is their job. What I would like you to do is to vote for this bill if you agree with what we're saying, or we would like to have another meeting so we can come in again and brief you or your staff on more details around this critical issue. That's your call-to-action.

That's your ask, period.

So you are running through six key steps:

- 1. Your issue
- 2. Your position
- 3. Your arguments
- 4. The facts
- 5. The story and
- 6. The ask

If you take this outline, the "5-3-5 T Framework," and you use it at the federal level, you can easily get a meeting with your lawmaker.

If you take this outline and use it at the state level, the same thing applies to whether you want to talk to a member of the assembly in your state legislature or a state senator.

If you take this same outline and you present it to your local council member, you will be at the head of the line. You will be concise. You'll be succinct. You will have clear communication with them, and they'll respect you for the fact that you did your homework.

You'll notice no shouting involved, no sign-waving, no marching, no screaming, no waiting in line, no standing around, no writing op-eds, no talk radio, just a clear template and framework for your proposed piece of legislation.

Narrowly defined, very specific, and in a language that they understand.

I WANTED to share this with you because this gets you into the political game.

Instead of complaining and crying about what a politician is or is not doing or being so overwhelmed by all the possible choices, or media crosstalk, or only voting and thinking that's going to take care of everything, this framework gives you the actual steps you need to get clear on an issue, to go forward, build a coalition, propose something. If you want to go farther, you can then start building up a bigger audience of supporters who agree with you.

YOUR GOAL IS to get the politician in your corner, to care about, and act on your issue. As I mentioned earlier, you need a bill sponsor.

YOU NEED someone who will champion your bill on your behalf. You cannot go in and introduce legislation on your own. It doesn't work that way.

You need a member, a lawmaker, to do that for you. The more you arm them with the details of what needs to be done and what's important, how it affects your community, how you as an individual or you and your group or you and your small business and other companies have solved this problem or propose to solve the problem, the better off you will be.

In effect, you are going to have the same power as a government affairs pro or maybe even a lobbyist.

You are going to have the same ability as any person in a corporate government relations office who is going in with several supporters and saying, "Hey, look. Here's a problem. I figured this out. I would like to present this to you, this is what we think the answer is."

In the end, maybe you will be one of the lucky ones who gets your bill written up by a member of Congress. You have it in committee or get a law named after you, and at least, you've gone so far as to actually have it in a legislative chamber.

At this point, you are now far ahead of the crowd.

You're far ahead of those who do nothing, sit back, and say, "There's no way to make a difference or effect change." Or they keep moaning about the sad state of partisan politics.

THIS IS the way to make a change. This is the way to have your voice heard.

. . .

THIS IS the way to begin to influence policy at any level of government and to be clear about what you think is important.

This will work for any issue as long as you do your homework. So I want you to feel comfortable playing with this. I want you to send us an email if you have questions about it.

I will include links at the end of this chapter where you can look at the platform, ask questions, learn more, take a look at some of our videos, get free training, move forward and hopefully begin to make a change in your neighborhood so that you can improve your community, influence your country, and impact the world.

GOOD LUCK and welcome to the game of politics, where you have transformed your life from apathy to engagement and empowerment.

REVIEW

If you liked this book, please fee free to leave an honest review. Just a line or two would be very helpful. I want you to know that I will definitely read your review. Thanks so much. Here are the links.

The Political Game

US
 http://www.amazon.com/review/create-review?&
asin=B07DT3T2S1

Goodreads
 https://www.goodreads.com/review/new/40594347-the-
political-game

Author's Direct Audio Book
 https://shop.authors-direct.com/products/the-political-game-
engage-and-transform-your-life-from-apathy-to-empowerment?
_pos=1&_sid=2c2548bac&_ss=r

ALSO BY JOHN THIBAULT

How to Change a Law Official Book Trailer

Preview: This book is a do-it-yourself manual for voters, small business owners, lobbyists, and policy advocates who want to take political action, influence leaders and change laws.

Once you understand the power of lobbying, you will be able to improve your community, influence leaders, and impact the world.

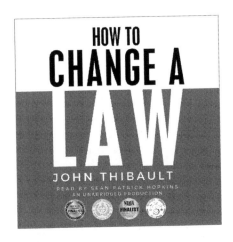

How To Change A Law offers insight, actionable tools, and strategies that will lead you to becoming an active Citizen Legislator who realizes that their participation in public policy matters.

We are at a turning point in our politics; everyone needs to get involved, come together, build coalitions, fund initiatives, and intelligently pursue their agenda.

How to Change a Law

How to Change a Law (Audible)

ABOUT THE AUTHOR

John Thibault is an award winning author and the founder and CEO of Silicon Valley startup, iLobby. He wrote the #1 International best-seller, bestseller "How to Change a Law," "Sway" and "The Political Game."

Previously he served in government affairs at MCA/Universal. He was also the first VP of business development and marketing at eBay and the first VP of marketing at Financial Engines.

He has been published in Association News, Manufacturing Today, CEO for High Growth Ventures and Millennial Magazine, and been interviewed on Amazon TV, and numerous radio affiliates for ABC, CBS, and NBC, podcasts and recently served on a panel for the "Tales of the Cocktail" Foundation.

He holds a Bachelor's degree from Ryerson University and an MFA from UCLA. He is a two-time cancer survivor, enjoys skiing and lives with his wife and three children in Northern California.

"If you've found this book useful, please consider leaving a short review on Amazon."

ABOUT ILOBBY

iLobby is an online platform that makes it easy for voters, small businesses, and trade associations to take political action by engaging in public policy.

iLobby connects voters with lobbyists to change laws.

People use iLobby to debate issues, seek resolution to political problems in the world or their community, and to discover, share, and express what is important to them.

facebook.com/ilobby.co
twitter.com/ilobbyco
instagram.com/ilobby.co

AWARDS

How To Change a Law

- **Gold Medal Winner**, Readers' Favorite Awards, 2017
- **Finalist,** 14th Annual American Book Fest, 2017
- Finalist, 11th Annual National Indie Excellence Book Awards, 2017
- Runner-Up, San Francisco Book Festival, 2017

iLobby

- **Finalist**, Community of Democracies "Annual Democracy Contest," 2016 Warsaw, Poland
- Quarterfinalist, Pepperdine University Most Fundable Companies, 2020

BONUS LINKS

- Web
- Twitter
- Twitter 2
- Facebook
- Blog
- Linked In
- Medium
- Instagram
- Quora
- YouTube
- iTunes Podcast
- Free Online Course
- Email Us

FREE STUFF

- 6 Things Politicians Want to Know
- 6 Reasons Why Congress Won't Listen To You
- Chet Campanella Story
- Free Online Interactive Course

SHARE YOUR STORY

If you have a story about how you changed a law, we would love to read it. It could be at the local, state or any level of government. We just ask that it be true, personal, and please keep it under 1200 words.

If your story is accepted, we may include it in a future version of How to Change a Law. Readers find these stories empowering, and it helps them believe that they can make a difference.

Simply email it to us with your contact information to support@ilobbyco.com

Please do not be discouraged if you do not hear back from us right away, as this can take time. If you do not hear from us within 90 days, chances are it is not right for us at this time.

Made in the USA
Middletown, DE
21 March 2024

51421170R00038